Between Two Worlds

Between Two Worlds

by Juliette 'Goldiebear' Margold

BearManor Media
2025

Between Two Worlds

Copyright © 2025 Juliette 'Goldiebear' Margold

Published in the United States of America by:

BearManor Media

1317 Edgewater Dr. #110
Orlando, FL 32804

bearmanormedia.com

Printed in the United States.

Typesetting and layout by PKJ Passion Global

ISBN–979-8-88771-685-5

PLAYLIST

I Don't Want to Be - Gavin Degraw

Don't Cry - Guns and Roses

Shake it out - Florence + The Machine

Cher - Jesse James

Cher - Bang Bang

Gotye - Somebody that I used to know

Ellie Goulding - Anything Could Happen

Heart - Alone

Candlebox (too many songs to list)

Skunk and Anansie - Secretly, Hedonism, Weak

Madonna - Bad Girl

The soundtrack to Lost Boys the movie

The soundtrack to Bugsy Malone

Luke Combs

Tracy Chapman

Pink (so many songs)

Imagine Dragons

Chinchilla - Little Girl Gone

Garth Brooks (too many good songs)

Chris Stapleton

People I would like to have dinner with just to chat about their music or acting I enjoyed

Pink (Alecia Moore) - *Your music has helped me through life in ups and downs.*

Guns and Roses Slash and Axl - *Your music got me through some hard times.*

Oprah Winfrey - *you interviewed my dad on September 17, 1982.*

Shonda Rhimes - *I am a huge fan of Grey's Anatomy.*

Ryan Murphy - *I would love you to do a mini-series on my life.*

Stevie Nicks - *just because you are awesome.*

Tracy Chapman - *your music is amazing.*

Rona Barrett - *you interviewed my father. I just wanted to let you know none of his daughters went into the porn industry.*

Acknowledgments

Thank you to my amazing mom Linda Hamilton. We miss you. 03/28/2017

Thank you to my daughter and husband for all your support.

Thank you to my amazing friends Missi and Kim for your support.

Thank you to Nicole for reading the chapters and supporting me.

Thank you to Rebecca for always being up for reading chapters and giving me honest feedback.

Thank you to Connor, we will definitely work on the podcast in 2025.

Thank you to my awesome sisters for all your support.

Thank you to my amazing ghostwriter, Sonny Malone.

Thank you Quinten Tarantino for making my father relevant again.

Thank Antoni for all the laughs and for listening to me.

Thank you to all my amazing friends.

1. One Day At Costco

No one has a crystal ball or timeline for when your parents are going to pass away. I had always wondered if Bill, my dad, died, how would I ever know. I had no contact with my father for five years, which was mutual on both sides. Most kids don't call their dads by their first name but I can explain. Most dads aren't porn stars. I suppose hearing me call him "daddy" might have been weird for him. He was probably called that in many of his 250 adult films.

It was a cool, slightly overcast, day in Los Angeles and my daughter was in preschool for the morning. I had a couple of hours before she needed to be picked up so I went to my favorite place, Costco, to sit in a rocking chair and check Facebook. It always relaxed me to be in the middle of the constantly moving crowd with the smell of pizza and $1.50 hot dogs. I was rocking gently, scrolling on my phone, and that was when I saw the post. I don't remember who posted it. The post said they needed the next of kin. I stopped rocking and the world around me fell silent.

I was not ready for the emotions that would come up with the events that would follow Bill's death. Somehow, I arrived at Bill's place, calling my husband to tell him what was happening. I do not even remember who picked up my daughter. But all of a sudden, Bill's friends flooded his Facebook online telling him how much they loved him and how great he had been. They spoke about a man I barely knew. I was shocked he seemed so beloved.

Bill's apartment was disgusting. Like, shoes sticking to the floor type of disgusting. My dad was not a decent housekeeper in any sense of the word and the place smelled. He had cats and with one whiff you knew it. The back of the 80's camelback orange flowered couch was still lined with teddy bears. They were all slightly grey with a thin film of dust and neglect. He had pictures of himself with other performers tacked haphazardly on the walls. Somewhere a cat meowed. I hated standing in the space and kept going out the open door just to get a breath of clean air.

Friends of Bill's were there, Amber, Mara, and Brian Sebastian, to help organize and handle things. As I barely knew these people, I talked to the police officer who arrived and I kept gulping that fresh air. My husband arrived two hours later.

The coroner who was sent was a small man and my husband and Brian had to help carry Bill's body down the stairs. I was not really into seeing a dead body, no matter who it was, so I was glad for the help. I signed papers with shaking hands as my phone was starting to blow up. A memorial was being planned in his honor so fast it made my head spin. My ex-stepmother Drea called me. I was not in the right head space to speak with anyone since all my energy was on my mother who was in the hospital fighting acute myeloid leukemia. I will get to that later. My world had turned on a dizzying axis and I was simply trying to keep two feet on the ground. I took baby steps throughout the next couple of weeks.

The memorial was another whirlwind. It took place on January 29, 2017. One thing about the San Fernando Valley was that it was hot even in the middle of winter. The event was set up in the backyard of one of Bill's friend's houses. There was a folding table strewn with bottles that looked like a bar. A clear plexiglass podium had been erected with a microphone attached. I watched people set out teddy bears and awards that meant nothing to me but were obviously cornerstones in Bill's life. Some people passed, petted a bear, maybe sniffed a little, and dabbed an eye then eyed the bar and a second empty table that was waiting for food.

The bagpipes were startling. I was sure I was dreaming but there were actual bagpipes. Then the doves. Something else that just seemed surreal and I was sure I could hear my father laughing at the pageantry of it all. It was like some minor monarch had died and the townspeople were pulling out the stops.

One man in a loud Hawaiian shirt spoke first. His voice boomed over the small crowd and said his fond farewell. Then he became the master of ceremonies and was lord over who would speak next. Next to him stood Amber in dark sunglasses, her large breasts threatening to spill out of her top. The Hawaiian shirt, Herschel Savage, told a story about shaking Bill's hand after Bill had eaten a messy lunch without utensils. Someone's phone went off. Amber was looking around for the next speaker.

Herschel suddenly pointed to me and introduced me, saying my name. I know he was speaking to me but the words were not coming together in my head. Somehow I made my way to the podium on wobbly legs.

I tried my best to hide under a dark hat and dark glasses. I knew I was the 'next of kin' but I felt completely out of place. I had a water bottle tucked under my arm and my phone in my hand as if they would protect me. I had no idea what to even say. I looked out at the expectant faces that didn't know me from a hole in the wall. Most were still circling the empty table waiting for the food like it was a game of musical chairs.

"I just really wanted to say thank you to everyone who loved my father. Some of you knew about me. Some of you didn't. I was Goldie Bear because it was on my birth certificate. Bill was very excited about that."

As I spoke, Amber tried to step in as MC to dictate what order people were going to speak. Herschel gently shut her down, their hushed argument throwing me even more off balance. Somehow, I kept talking.

"He loved bears. Great aunt was Golda." I babbled, looking for an exit. "I just want to say thank you for the outpouring. Thank you to everyone who has contributed and helped and just loved the man. I think he'd be amazed and excited about how many people showed up and how many people loved him. He loved everyone. Everyone was his kid. And he was Papa Bear."

The Amber and Herschel argument got heated and I wanted to scream. I just wanted out.

"So, that's all I want to say. Thank you." I bolted from the spotlight like a squirrel hearing an oncoming car.

I watched from the sidelines as one by one people made their way to the podium. Fingerprints were left on the clear plastic with each tear and tribute. One thing struck me as more odd than this whole affair.

As Herschel spoke, loudly and with authority, suddenly he stopped. Frozen. They all did. As if they were robots and someone just pulled a giant plug. Then I saw it and heard it. An airplane was flying overhead. It was explained to me years later that adult actors when filming stop for plane sounds. They stop mid-thrust and go still like a deer in a forest hearing a cracking branch. Once the sound is gone, the director tells them to continue and they go on like nothing happened. It's a film sound thing. It still baffles me.

As the people spoke and moved on, Amber once again was trying to keep things moving. Lunch had been delivered. I watched the crowd begin to hover over the barbeque like vultures. The real star of the show had arrived. Sure Bill was dead, but lunch was being provided! It made me think of Dicken's 'A Christmas Carol' when the money men are trying to decide whether or not to attend Scrooge's funeral. They decide they will indeed attend. One man says; "*I don't mind going if a lunch is provided.*"

Somewhere during all of this, a GoFundMe was set up to cover the costs of the memorial and other expenses. Someone slithered up to me and graciously offered to handle everything. Money was generously donated but when I needed it, the man who set everything up tried to keep it. Bill had fans that slipped in at this time and tried to claim that I was only here for the money. They had no conception that I was the man's daughter. Most of them didn't even know Bill had kids. Somehow, I was cast as the villain. The GoFundMe guy (whose name doesn't even deserve to be spoken here) proceeded to call me all sorts of names and hurl insults at me online.

Karma is bitch. The man would die 7 months later. I couldn't care less about the money.

2. How I Lost My Mother

My mother was an amazing woman and someone I spoke to daily later in our lives. She was a social service worker for Los Angeles County for 37 years. Our relationship had been turbulent throughout my childhood but as I became an adult, I believe it got a lot better. We were able to talk more. My mother was capable of helping the irrational side of my brain be more rational. She went to doctor appointments with me because I was a hypochondriac and she would hold my hand. She talked me down off some ledges with grace and patience.

She listened to me and gave her opinion even when I did not want to hear it. But, she was always honest. On February 29, 2016, my mother took her first fall. Linda, my mother, had always been healthy. My friends and I would joke about how she would live forever. Going to the gym 7 days a week, eating very healthy, and walking 3 miles a day is what made Mom happy.

We were on our normal walk to Costco. We liked strolling the aisles and seeing what samples were out each time we went. No matter if we liked it or not, we always took the sample. Each time we would decide if it was Good Sample Day or Bad Sample Day.

After what we deemed it a Good Sample Day, we walked through the sunny parking lot to our car. Out of nowhere, she stepped up to a planter box and tripped falling face-first into the asphalt. When she lifted her head and I saw blood, I had to call 911 for the first time. She has gashed open her forehead.

Who knew I would call 2 more times that year?

Mom was taken to Kaiser West Los Angeles and received 12 stitches. Not the best ending for Good Sample Day.

A little back story; my mom had surgery in December 2015 for unknown reasons. Speculation was her appendix had burst in June

2015 but at this point when the surgeon went in it was exploratory surgery. The results came back and thank god it was not cancer. They had taken a section of her colon and 21 lymph nodes out.

March 9th, 2016. My mother started having stomach pains and stayed home from the gym which was very very rare. My sister picked Mom up and took her to the ER.

March 11th, 2016. She was admitted and given a nasal gastric tube trying to figure out what was going on.

March 16th,2016. My mother was taken into surgery at this point her platelets were going down and they had to transfusion 2 units of platelets before surgery. I remember the exact words of the surgeon; *'We are not sure what we are going to find and she could be in ICU.'*

As I grew into an adult and mother, she always was my stability. With not having my father around and not being able to rely on anyone but her or myself so watching her take her last breath was the hardest thing I have ever had to do.

If you only knew my year

My dad took his last breath on January 18th,2017. Gone from a heart attack.

My mom took her last breath on March 28th, 2017.

After a little less than a year from a battle with AmL. She had it twice.

My friend's mom who was a good friend of my mother's went to heaven on April 24th, 2017

My sister-in-law lost her mother on March 14th,2017.

My car window was broken on June 10th,2017 with my 3 1/2 daughter, 7-year-old niece, and my best friend in the car. In a hotel valet parking lot. The parking lot had no cameras.

Please, let the rest of the year be boring please…please.

3. Immaturity

My father produced 3 girls; all born in September. All Virgos. I was the last one, the youngest. The first two were step-sisters from other women.

Out of the three of us, I was the one who got the name Goldie Bear. Because of Jewish tradition (on my mother's side), my middle name became Golda after my grandmother. Therefore 'Goldie Bear'. My father created a fancy handmade declaration of my arrival. Seems I was the only one who got this honor.

My mother was born on November 8, 1944. Her parent's names were Teddy and Max Kleinberg. She would spend the first 15 years of her life being sexually molested by her father. Once out of high school, she decided to go to college and she studied for her bachelor's in history.

My mother tried out for the Peace Corps but wasn't accepted. Then she met Ron Hamilton, her first husband. He was an alcoholic and my mother decided to leave him. That is when she met my father, Bill Margold. They met when they were parole officers at a place called McLaren Hall. They never married but she wanted a child. Bill has said in many interviews that he was simply the donor. He explained up front he wasn't down for being a father. My mother agreed but still wanted a kid. She had me and Bill went on with his life. That's what made that hand-made announcement odd. For someone who didn't want me, he sure made a big deal about me being born.

My mother and I lived in a two-bedroom, one-bath bungalow in Culver City. I had my own bedroom but often slept in my mother's bed from a very young age. I thought I would be safe there but I had horrible nightmares and would kick my mother violently. With that, I was in therapy from age 5.

With that, I finally figured out something very important. My father left when I was three. His life would be dedicated to helping others in the industry, the innocent, those with no voice. With my father gone, my mother dove into her social work headfirst, often forgetting to come up for air. She dedicated her life to helping others, the innocent, those with no voice. I was cut adrift but neither of them realized it. I was screaming for their attention but they were busy saving the world.

I often accompanied my mom to her work before I was handed off to babysitters and neighbors. I remember going to pick up newborn drug addict babies from the hospital. I would see their innocent faces, tiny hands reaching out for anyone to hang onto, to take care of them. I often begged my mom to take them home with us. No one had been there to save me, I was sure I was the right person to take care of these children. I was seven.

I spent a lot of time in my mom's office talking with the workers while taking premature baby diapers for my cabbage patch dolls. I would go on visitation that my mom was supervising. It took all

I had to keep my hands to myself and not take the baby from the home. Then bump into her clients on the public busses.

When my mother had to handle the remote hotline, I imagined myself as a social worker. However, I knew I would have every single person on the other end of that phone in my home in a heartbeat. That phone rang a lot. I backed away from a social worker career path. I was still seven.

My mother worked up to six days a week. Also, she was obsessed with weight, hers and mine, so she went to the gym six days a week, sometimes seven, for up to three hours a day. With her work and gym schedule, I spent most of my time with the family next door. They were like my babysitters. I called them the Latin Catholics.

I spent more time with them than my own mother or sisters. There were four of them ranging in age from ten years older than me to the youngest being close to my age. As I craved siblings and a family, I emulated what they did to blend in and fit in. I ate the food they had and learned about make-up and how to dress from the older ones. I learned about being social, how to have a boy like me, how to be pretty. I wasn't raised by a girly-girl mom so I watched the Latin Catholic girls to learn how to navigate the girl world. I thought if I did all that, I might be happy, might be my own person outside of the porn dad and restrictive mom.

Yet, when my mother was watching me, she watched me like a hawk. She watched everything I put in my mouth as I had an obese aunt and mom didn't want me to suffer the same fate. Mom would constantly tell me to go run around the block and say '*Don't eat that*' if I reached for anything she didn't approve of.

Being dyslexic and diagnosed with ADHD, I was put on Ritalin for 3 years which really helped me learn and stay focused. My mother did some research and I was sent to an amazing school called Park Century. There were only an average of seven kids in a class and it helped me immensely. After those three years, I was mainstreamed into the public school setting not really understanding how to be social, even with my Latin Catholic girl lessons. It was a bit overwhelming to be thrown into a classroom with 25 kids. I was at a complete loss and did my best not to drown.

The summer before 8th grade, my mother found this pamphlet at work. It was a summer camp for kids. Specifically what they used to call a 'fat camp'. As I was rampant with hormones, my weight fluctuated wildly. When mom suggested the camp, I went without much struggle. I actually enjoyed it! I went for two summers! My meals were portioned and there was all this activity. I lost close to twenty pounds each time. I never saw it as a punishment it was a fun summer camp. My mom's love language was working out.

I had a lot of good childhood memories of weight loss camp. I finally felt somewhat accepted by my peers. I also have a wonderful memory of going to the beach when I was seven. Swimming in the ocean without a care in the world was very calming to me. My friend Chloe and I did cartwheels in the low tide, laughing and giggling like the carefree children we were.

Another time, I got to pick out my cat from the pound and named her 'Meawdonna". Even though Bill was not a dad, we would go out for Chinese food to a restaurant on Pico Blvd called Chung King and have three flavor sizzling rice soup and Peking Duck. These are the childhood memories that make me smile. The feeling of happiness, the taste of the soup, the smell of the ocean, and the softness of my cat and hearing her purr. Random thoughts from when my childhood was happy. It's nice to look back and not see it all bad.

Mom became a vegetarian briefly and banned sugary things from the house. She controlled what she felt she could control. When I was at the Latin Catholics's house, I discovered what sugary snacks and sodas were. Also, burritos. However, I was also to be looked down upon. What colored who I was to them was my father, the evil porn star. The judgment came from the Latin Catholic's mother.

Their mother often said I was a 'bad influence'. This made no sense to me. I was the nice kid! How was I the bad guy? Just because my dad did porn, I was painted with the 'bad seed' brush.

Then something dawned on me. When I was seven, one of the older Latin Catholic girls walked into my bedroom without knocking. I was masturbating. I wasn't one hundred percent sure what I was doing I only knew it felt good. Of course, that news whipped around the family like wildfire. According to my mother, I had been "eroticized". By my father? By his business? I don't know, she never explained it beyond that. I was a human discovering my body and had no idea I was doing anything deemed 'bad'.

I was six or seven years old when I realized my father was a porn star or someone famous at least. We were out for breakfast and someone saw the teddy bear I was holding, Mr. Stubbs. They said *'Oh, I know that bear'.*

It was my mother's idea that I get to know my dad. Why? Who knows. I don't know what Bill's reaction was to that conversation. I just remember being dropped off at his apartment, or he would come to get me in an old red van that my mother had given him. The van was part of his personality and later I would discover everyone associated that van with my father.

When I would arrive at his place, I would be met with the naked bodies displayed as artwork on his wall. They were everywhere. The pictures often included him smiling with a half-naked or totally nude smiling female. In those pictures, Bill and the girl always seemed very happy. Then again, in some pictures it would be just him enjoying a meal or smiling wide, laughing at a silent joke. Some pictures were framed, and some were simply tacked up with push pins and curling at the edges. There was also no rhyme or reason for this decoration. It seemed like Bill saw an empty spot and filled it with his smiling face. Along with that were the teddy bears that crammed every corner of the place. Bears and shelves crammed with tapes of golden age porn along with awards and certificates. There was no room for me. There was no room for anyone except for who he wanted to let in.

Bill was called 'Papa Bear' in the industry. I think he gave himself that name. Bill called me "kid," but he called everyone, including his costars and friends, "kid." I was welcome to visit him, but it wasn't because he needed father-daughter time. Again, this was my mother's idea. I often wondered if this was her way to get me to not spend so much time with the Latin Catholic girls. Or maybe my mother needed some alone time for herself without worrying about where I was or what I was eating.

At Bill's place, it was abundantly clear that he wouldn't change anything for me, his unintended family. It was as if I were a pet he couldn't decide on. Should he let the dog stay or drop her off at the shelter? I knew I wasn't the product of love. My mom and Bill met on a blind date and Bill's words were blunt.

"Your mother wanted a child, so I performed. I never wanted kids. The porn industry is the only family I need." Bill once said.

That hurts as deep today as the day he said it to me but I will never admit it out loud. If I am in a therapy session and need to access some deep feelings, I bring up those words just to feel them twist my stomach. They are a gut punch yet a key to unlocking anything I need to access to. I suppose you would call them a 'turning point' or 'touchstone' for all the wrong reasons.

Above the couch in his apartment, there was a poster in a frame. Seemed out of all the other pictures, this one was special and deserved a real frame. It was a a group of scantily clad girls pushing up a flag, Iwo Jima style as if to mimic the famous World War II photograph. I would learn later this was his true mission for his 'kids' in the industry. He called it PAWS (Protecting Adult Welfare). He was their Papa Bear. If any wayward porn soul needed rent, food, or a shoulder to cry on, Bill was there with whatever they needed. I don't think I had a name for Bill's profession until I was nine or ten. Porn.

My first real memory of my dad was taking a bath with him at 2 years old. At 3 years old, my sister and he moved out of the house to West Hollywood. That is when he brought Drea into our lives. There are several interviews with my father where he said he hated Drea. He married her so she would divorce him. I guess he thought this was funny.

At 5 years old I was roller skating in West Hollywood and hanging out at the park in Coldwater Canyon while my dad played football. He played every week and hated when he had to miss a game. My being around him often cramped his style. Even though, once, I helped him set up for the FOXX awards, which he produced, displaying photos of black men engaged in anal sex. After football, it was lunch at McDonalds with fish sandwiches.

By age 7, my father chose not to be in my life and said kids should not be around the porn industry. Drea would give Bill his anticipated divorce. A year or two later, I was thrown right back into his life again. This time he was with a woman named Viper or Stephanie. This woman other people in the industry called '*The Love of Bill's Life*'. She had red hair, nipple piercings, and a dragon tattoo that wrapped around her entire body. I remember asking my father if he was going to marry her too and he laughed.

If we were not at the apartment, the visits were at a house in Coldwater Canyon that was used to shoot porn. One hot summer night I was with Viper and Bill at this house. The place had a pool and hot tub. I heard light splashing in the water and walked out to find a small pile of clothes and Viper naked paddling in the clear water.

"You wanna come in?" She asked. She was not self-conscious at all. She stood in the water as her breasts bounced right at the surface.

"I don't have a swimsuit," I muttered.

"I haven't owned a swimsuit since the early '70s," Viper said as if it was nothing and floated on her back.

I might have hesitated but then I stripped down naked and jumped in. The cool water gave me goosebumps. There was nothing sexual about our swim. In fact, after I took off my clothes, I didn't even think about the fact that we were both naked in public. Private backyard but still outside, exposed. I didn't feel shame attached to sex or attached to my body. That would come for me later.

Viper gave me my first pair of high heels at 10 and I loved them. I wore them around the house all the time. They had a slim black heel with plastic over the toe and fake rhinestones. I remember when the movie Pretty Woman came out at that point and I had a tight-fitting dress and my hooker heels. For some reason, I wanted to be a prostitute for Halloween. I wonder what ever happened to those shoes?

Before Viper, when I would visit my father, I would sleep in his bed. Since at home I often slept in my mother's bed, for me, this was a natural progression. Nothing bad ever happened to me, this was just the way it was in my life. Then dad got a girlfriend and I was relegated to the couch.

Viper. Viper. After Viper, he never had another girlfriend. She left him after five years. From what I've read, she moved clear across the country and disappeared. She was a snake. She was a bear. When they had sex, either in the apartment or the canyon house. I would be sleeping in the living room. I could hear them. When it got quiet, I knew what was coming next.

Viper got up after sex, walked through the house to the guest shower, and cleaned up. Why she never used the other shower is beyond me. When she was done, she would walk right back to the bedroom. For some reason, this memory is burned into my brain. Too many times when I close my eyes I see that tattoo slither through the room and back.

As I grew older, I began to notice a gaping discrepancy in my father's behavior. To my sisters and I, he let us know he had no designs nor desires to play the role of "dad" in our lives. But to the porn girls he worked with, he was an advocate. In fact, he became known as a pioneer in the porn industry throughout his career, working prior to the rulings that protected porn and adult entertainers with the First Amendment.

Bill cared about what Bill cared about and that was Bill and Bill's interests. "Narcissist" doesn't scratch the surface of Bill's egotistical nature. I knew these facts, had heard my mother affirm them, had observed them myself, and yet … I longed to be loved by him. I longed to be worth fighting for like the girls he worked with were worth fighting for. He called his home a "safe haven" for all these other girls. But for me, his home became a place where I helped him arrange pictures of men having sex for an award show.

When I was 12, I wrote Bill a letter. I tried to muster up all the disdain and anger I could and I laid it all on the line. I told him he was a terrible father and that I hated him. I wanted to take him on Donahue or Geraldo and humiliate him. I had done all I could to be his daughter but I was hitting a brick wall. Try as I might, he didn't want a daughter. He didn't want me to look up to him, lean on him or need him. I wanted him to show *some* kind of emotion. He wasn't capable of showing emotion to me. As I am dyslexic, I often get letters and sometimes words mixed up. Bill noticed.

"Your grammar is shit," was his only response to my letter.

To deliver this famed letter, I made my older sister take us to our usual Chinese restaurant to meet our dad. Here is how Bill remembered it:

When Viper was starting to disintegrate, I had a meeting with my real kids at a Chinese restaurant on Washington Blvd. – on Washington and Centinela. I told them that I would not be able to pay attention to them anymore. I explained to them that I was completely involved with what Viper was going through and that I could not, in any way, shape, or form, rationalize giving any attention to anybody else but Viper.

However, I told them, "If you ever need me for anything, you know where I'm at."

WILLIAM MARGOLD,

INTERVIEWED BY CHARLES ZIGMAN on July 14, 2009.

I never knew the real reason was Viper. I was sure he just didn't want anything to do with us, which was also true. I wanted that caring and love he was giving to Viper in her time of need.

By the time I was 12 years old, I felt that I had lived an entire life. I was angry and going through puberty and had been in and out of therapy thanks to my mom. Mom was trying her best to contain my irrational hormones and the basics of raging puberty. One therapist was named Bob. I will never forget Bob. My sister and I both saw Bob. One day Bob sat me down and he had on a very stern look. His exact words were: '*If you do not get happy you will end up commuting suicide*'. Just what a confused 12-year-old needs to hear. Thanks, Bob.

As I was clinging to my mother for stability, puberty rearing its ugly head, my weight fluctuating, and my hormones doing whatever the hell they wanted, my mother enacted the ultimate betrayal as I was drowning daily. She got a boyfriend.

I had no idea then why this upset me so badly but I remember getting her diaphragm and throwing it out the window onto the front lawn. Here I am still overweight, before fat camp, hating myself, needing a father figure, and then this boyfriend comes along. I don't even remember his name but it doesn't matter. I had been dealt a heavy parental blow and sharing my mother at that time was simply not an option. As I said, completely irrational 12-year-old here.

When I did threaten to kill myself (way to go, Bob), my mom sent me to more therapy. But not good old Bob. I told the new doctor that it was my mother who needed the help.

At 18, I moved out.

4. An Open Letter to the Latin Catholics

Dear ex-best friends that I consider family my sisters,

We grew up next door to one another.

We played Barbies. We took the car out. 13-year-olds doing fun and stupid things.

The amount of time I spent at your house and eating cereals and diet sodas that were not allowed in my house was immeasurable. The time you spent at my house eating fresh fruits and putting our dog in the bathroom due to your fears, was also a lot. The struggles as we became pre-teens and then teenagers, we struggled together.

I considered you my sisters.

The times you spent speaking to my mother asking her advice no matter if you want to hear it or not. My mother was always truthful to you. The amount of blame your mother put upon me for your faults. The hurtful words from you when my mother was sick. I planned a trip you didn't agree with, how dare I go away when my mother was ill. Your judgment was because of your own failings, not mine.

The thought that I was interfering with your child's raising when you were so blind and could not see the issue staring you in the face. The fights we had that went on without speaking for years.

Your judgment was thinking I would never have to work again if my mother passed away. What I would give to have my mother back. No amount of money was worth it watching my mother taking her last breath and knowing there was nothing I could do. I am living a much better life without my false sisters, you. It was not an easy childhood being diagnosed at 7 with dyslexia and ADHD. I was put on Ritalin for 3 years which really helped me learn and stay focused.

The Latin Catholic neighbors turned mean. '*Juliet, don't come over, you're a bad influence*'. Your mother blamed me for your issues. As adults, you blame me for your issues, your children's issues.

My sister took you to get your first AIDS test. My mother listened to all your woes and problems because your Catholic mother couldn't hear anything.

The last time I spoke to both of you was in November 2016. The best thing I could do was to get them both the fuck out

Yours,
Juliette

5. Sex Around The World

January 1981 - *Rona Barrett interviewed me (Bill), she asked me if I had [natural] children. I said, "Yeah, anyone can have kids, that takes no talent." She said, "Would you allow your daughter to be in the X-rated business?" I said, "Yeah, I really don't care what she does. It would be hypocritical of me to tell her what to do when she turns eighteen. In fact," I told her, "I'll work with her myself!"*

She was amazed! I said, "Well, no, I'm not really going to fuck my own daughter."

==========

I am going to assume something about the general public and people reading this book. They would land on this chapter as they flipped through it to see if they wanted to read it. A chapter about and titled 'sex'. It might be where they start.

They might be disappointed.

Even though I did discover masturbation at a young age, I developed much like any other young girl would in a suburban world. Let me say here and now: I was never molested. I was never on a porn set or exposed to the porn world at a young age. Ever.

I wanted to be anyone but me. Who wanted to like a girl who had a parent who was a porn star? The confession of Dad's world was almost an apology every time I said it. When I started when I started becoming sexually active I was prepared to be judged simply because my father was a porn star.

I didn't have my first kiss until I was 13. After that, I would play games at parties for a couple of years. More kissing and giggles like any young person at that age. My first blow job happened when I was 16 years old. It was with a boy I had a crush on for a year. At that point in my life, I was overweight and did not feel good about my looks. The love of my life was drunk and kept pestering me for a blow job. Not knowing anything about anything I asked for a condom. He gave me one, I put it on him and blew him. The coating on the outside of it made my lips numb. I am not even sure he came. He denied we did anything for the rest of his life and I told anyone who would listen.

I started Santa Monica High School in 1990 and graduated in 1994.

My freshman year was probably the worst. I did not really understand the meaning of the word 'popular' and sort of swam upstream against the popularity current. Literally, I joined the swim team to make friends.

This is also where I would discover traveling. I had never been farther than my own backyard and my father's place when my sister started teaching English in Seoul, Korea. It might as well have been Oz and I wanted to go see the Wizard. I am not sure where this idea even came from, I only knew I wanted to visit my sister. On my own. I was in the 10th grade.

I was 15 years old and had never been on a plane by myself. I was giving myself a real adventure. It was a Delta airline from LAX to SFO to Portland Oregon to Seoul Korea. I remember all those connections all these years later. With my luck, just before the trip, I had gotten the flu. Thankfully, by the time the day came to leave, I was over it but the cough hung on and refused to leave. Still, I made my way onto the plane clutching my bright yellow sports Walkman with a single of Guns and Roses 'Don't Cry'. I played it on repeat for hours.

Now, this was what we now call 'back in the day' and the plane seats still had a little silver square that flipped to reveal an ashtray. I was still fighting this cough as cigarette smoke from first class drifted throughout the plane. The nice couple next to me flagged down the stewardess and cups of hot tea magically arrived right on cue.

I remember landing in Korea and when I got off the plane, there were armed men in the terminal. The sight of the guns made me slow my step as I all but gawked at them, then hurried along to baggage claim. My sister had to educate me regarding North Korea then things made sense. Exposing myself to this new culture was all I needed to know I wanted to travel. I wanted to make sure I had a job that would allow me this luxury of seeing the world and getting paid for it. But first, I had to finish high school.

The next blow job I gave was in 1993. I was a senior in high school. I had yet another crush. It was a summer house party and there was a lot of alcohol around so I was as drunk as the next person, and my crush who wanted a blow job. We slipped out to the garden behind the house. Inside, the loud party faded as we got further and further away from the music and people. It wasn't some romantic moonlit night. I could still hear the traffic over the stone wall from the freeway. I remember I stayed standing up and didn't even go on my knees. I blew him but when he came in my mouth, I didn't swallow. I kept my mouth closed and walked back into the party with his cum in my mouth. I kept it there for a while and realized the power I had. I had power.

Fast forward to the present and ironically I watch a lot of porn. That took me quite a long time to come to terms with. Here was the industry that my father chose over me and I was watching it. No, I never watched one of Bill's films. Once I got over the hatred of the industry and grew up, I looked at porn with a different appreciation. Also, I got a vibrator and that sort of changed my whole world. With that amount of studying, my friends come to me for sex advice. I am the least judgemental person there is. *What should I try or what should I do with this? Or I don't like giving blowjobs. Do you have any, you know, suggestions?* I try to think of things I've seen in these porn films as well as my own experience to try and help.

I lost my virginity at 18. When I finished high school, I set my sights on college. I also chose a college that was as far away from my current world as possible. My mother wouldn't really allow me to go as fast as the East Coast, so Seattle was the next best thing. I wasn't running from anything that bad at this point I simply knew it was time for me to try life on my own, like any 18-year-old. It was time for me to see what choices I wanted to make for my life including what I ate and who I slept with. My mother and I went to Seattle to see the city and the college, Art Institute of Seattle. I was going to study to work in the travel industry. Seattle was far from home but I wanted to go a lot farther.

I started dating a guy pretty quickly once I was settled into the dorm system. He was alright but I really liked his roommate. Since this chapter is about sex, let's get back to that.

For some reason, Jeremy caught my interest. I remember making out with him and he was the first guy to ever go down on me I remember having an orgasm. I gave him my virginity. I don't think I had an orgasm during that first time. This felt like it was simply something to do, the next step in my sexual development. I'd kissed, and given blowjobs, this was next. He was nice about it and a good guy but obviously, the relationship served its purpose.

When I graduated in June of 1996, I got my real chance to bolt. After attending the Art Institute of Seattle, I decided I wanted to go out for my bachelor's. I found Johnson and Wales and Providence Rhode Island and decided to try it out without visiting. Figuring it was simply the farthest point. I got there and really disliked it. At this point, my mother's reach was still in play so clearly I had not gone far enough. She insisted I drop out and return to therapy to make sure college was exactly what I wanted to do with my life. If yes, she would still cover the costs. so I dropped out of college and my mother made me go back to therapy to decide if she was willing to send me back to college.

It didn't take long and as soon I was done with my mother's demand, I was in college in Florida studying the travel industry.

Spring of 1997, I moved to Florida to attend Schiller and met my first boyfriend. This is when I learned that I really like men from India. Also In Florida, I slept with a guy my roommate was also sleeping with. We discovered the meaning of the World's Smallest Penis.

I never really liked Florida so looked at the other campuses the college offered. My first stop was in London spring of 1999 with an awesome roommate.

Moving to London was really exciting because I had never gone and lived in another country by myself. I was a student! I would go to classes and then see the sights with my new friends, also students. We even went to the memorial for Princess Diana.

Then my boyfriend at the time came to visit me from Florida. We were trying to make things work and I was excited to show him my new life. Of course, we had sex. I had found this French Tickler thing to enhance our experience but somehow I got it stuck inside me. The freakout was fairly immediate.

I am in a foreign country and I need to get to a doctor., How do I even do that!? My mother is over six thousand miles away so of course I called her in a total panic. Eventually, I got to a doctor. After a quick exam, the diagnosis was *'you have a French tickler stuck inside you'*. Ah, modern medicine. Luckily, it was easily removed along with most of my dignity.

I broke up with the boyfriend and thought a fresh start was a good thing. I got a job in Turkey at a resort.

The only issue with Turkey is that I was hired as a hostess. This meant I was basically arm candy. I was there to entertain and look pretty. No, I never slept with anyone who hired me as a hostess. I was literally there as an accessory. I realized this was not what I went to college for.

Then, I met Ali. He was cute and a virgin. He was the first guy whose virginity I took. Without having to attend classes and only a job to be loyal to, I felt free. I liked sharing my sexual knowledge with Ali. I like to say he was fun to play with. I realized I was attracted to their innocence and wanted to help in a way. My way of reaching out to help the less fortunate, I suppose. Since I had planned on being there for only the summer, we broke up near the end of my time there. Neither of us wanted to try long distance and I was just starting on my own journey of self-discovery.

A blow job is probably one of my favorite things to do. When I am at my highest peak sexuality, I am thin. I feel good. I feel beautiful. But there are times that I let my vulnerability get in the way and I start eating. Eating is my emotional crutch. Eating makes me fat. Eating turns off my sexual side completely. So, when I was feeling down, instead of eating, I gave a blow job.

I took another guy's virginity when I returned to London. A very handsome boy, a sweet boy like Ali. I educated him. I was more than glad to lend a hand.

My roaming days ended in 2001 when I returned to the States and moved in with my mother.

I had not seen my father in years and for some reason, I was invited to the Foxe Awards in 2002. I felt good about it. I was feeling good, wearing a short skirt. I wanted my father's approval in any way I could get it. I thought looking good, much like the performers he was still rescuing, would do the trick.

At the show, I was bored out of my mind and my father barely said hello. I am not even sure he knew who I was at first. I had to stop myself from walking up to him and saying *'Hi, it's me. Your daughter.'* I watched a woman set her nipples on fire as people enjoyed cocktails. It was an entirely different world to anything I had ever seen. Now that I was a sexually active adult, I understood things better. Or thought I did.

I also thought I wanted to be a porn star.

One thing I did notice about my life when I was abroad. If I told anyone who my father was or that fact that he had been a porn star, it was met with a polite nod, maybe a polite shrug. But then the information was dropped. It simply wasn't important, My friends wanted to know about me and spend time with me, not the memory of my father's career.

When I returned to those states, the judgment came back in full force.

6. Welcome to the Swing World

With all my college explorations, after graduation, I dove into the fast lane of the swing world. Having been exposed to sex so early in life it was never presented as a bad thing, I felt ready to keep going. So, I did.

I dated a variety of men off Plenty of Fish. That was where I met, and here I'm going to call him, 'Swinger'.

We started dating and we got along well. We went to Paradise Cove in Malibu. Sort of fancy and right on the beach in its own private strip of sand. We talked so much that our food was all but forgotten. After the meal, we walked that small strip of beach and just kept getting to know each other.

He had lost his wife and was looking for companionship. I wanted to be there for him, and I figured I could be the one to fix him and make him whole again. I had that sort of 'save the world' complex, so we kept dating.

I will say he was not a great kisser. Amazing penis, but not a great kisser. I still thought I could fix him.

After a few dates, some make-out sessions and, of course, sex, he brought up the idea of a Swing Party. I have no idea if he did this with his deceased wife or if this was a new thing. However, the idea completely piqued my interest. It was a Halloween party at a private house. Nerves made my stomach clench as he drove us to the place. I remember keeping a hold of his hand as we walked into the home and turned into the living room. At first glance, it looked like any other party, but the lights were sort of low. As I stood there, I listened and heard the soft sounds of sex. Then as I squinted I saw a woman giving a man a blow job. It wasn't a costume party, it just happened on Halloween so there were no weird outfits with body parts coming through. Just people, enjoying each other. No judgment.

One by one, I learned the rules as we walked through the rooms. First, do not talk to any couple you are not attracted to. This made sense to me. I was open to the swing world but everyone has their limits. Swinging does not mean open season on everyone in the room. There needs to be an initial attraction, some sort of spark, or it won't be fun for anyone.

If you do find someone attractive, feel free to say hello and talk. Just get to know the person at least a little before you just dive in. Set some ground rules as you would with any sexual partner. This is a safe space.

No one will ever just grab you and start making out with you. This isn't that kind of scene. YOu see something you like, you ask. The Swing World is a very polite place. People have respect for each other and their perspective partners.

The Swing World is a place for safe play. Not marriage and relationships. If you are with a couple if will most likely be for that night. Maybe you might see them at another party. You will not be at their breakfast table the next day.

I also learned that fantasies are totally on the table in this world. I love giving blow jobs. I learned a lot from watching other women and I taught them just as much on how to please your partner. Once, I thought it would be hot to watch Swinger suck another man's cock. He agreed to give it a shot. I was right, it was hot. The guy we found to play with was more than happy to make my fantasy come true.

I've always considered myself bisexual so I got to play with a lot of women. They were always soft and more than happy to play with me. We'd make out, masturbate while people watched, sometimes a man would join us, or other times it was just me and other women. I love playing with fake boobs. For some reason, it just makes me laugh!

I think everyone should go to a swing party at least once. Whether you're just a voyeur or if you participate. Because you have to realize that it's okay to be that sexual in that open. You have to be able to be comfortable in your own skin.

Yes, I've been involved in orgies, threesomes, sometimes just watching. I was at my thinnest and happiest with my body, I would prowl through the parties wearing a fedora and sucking a lollipop. I was free, I was happy.

At each party, I was able to lose myself totally in the experience. I could dance. I could walk around with no top on. I could run around making out with different people. I could watch people having sex. I mean, to be honest, I really do think I would have gone into the industry at that point.

After the swing party, Swinger and I would go back to his condo and he would cook us dinner. He was a great cook. We might have sex again or just enjoy each other's company. There was no pressure either way, that was also very freeing to be that relaxed with someone I was sleeping with.

Then, Swinger got a girlfriend. As I said, swinging is not a relationship place so once I was in the Swing World with Swinger, I went from potential mate to plaything. I could respect that but I won't say it didn't hurt. I had become very fond of Swinger and our times at the parties. Then I also realized Swinger hadn't slept with any only one other woman at these parties besides me. Also, his wife's ashes were still in his home. He liked swinging but clearly, he wanted to return to being a homebody.

Of course, once he met the new girlfriend, me and the parties were off the table. Or so he told her. Swinger and I still slept together for some time.

For the record, yes I did take my husband to a swing party once or twice. But, the vibe was completely different. This wasn't just some guy I was dating, this was a man I said 'I do' to and wanted to have children with. Not that the parties were not fun, I think I had changed once I fell in love. I wanted to be that home-body now, home with my man.

7. Sugar Daddies

Sugar Daddy *(noun)*: *a rich older man who lavishes gifts on a young woman in return for her company or sexual favors.*

===============

Recently, I overheard my husband and a friend of his talking. They were having a random conversation so I didn't listen or anything. Until, the subject turned to the men's daughters, our daughter.

"Hell yeah, I'm going to protect her." My husband says.

"No older guys either. I don't want some old guy creeping around my little girl." The friend says.

I felt an odd pang of pure jealousy. What they were saying was all I had been craving my entire life: a father figure to protect me. It is something I never had, never will, and will probably always look for in my life. I've always wanted a Dad.

Sugar daddies, in my mind, seemed like the next logical step. I was working for a cruise line when I met Travel Agent.

We were simply doing normal business over the phone but something clicked. We would laugh and laugh as we got our business done. The call might even have gotten flirty, it probably did. I remember soon after our call I received a $300 gift card in the mail. All I had done was make the man laugh. Soon after, he asked me out to lunch.

He was attractive and older and I instantly fell into 'pleasing' mode. We never had sex, all I did was give him massages. I went from 'pleasing' to discovering my power. Give a massage, get a gift. I was starting to really rack up those gift cards.

Then I found the website SugarDaddy.com and created a profile. I still saw Travel Agent whenever he wanted to get together but

I also was ready to branch out. I was ready to find a Daddy to take care of me. On my terms.

I met Bob for my first really sugar daddy experience. He flew me to Las Vegas and I already felt like I was being taken care of. He booked a high-end hotel room, we saw a few shows. We ate at the finest restaurants and even got to spend time in the day spa. Of course, there was also the amazing sex. Of course, there was also the $300 shopping spree at Victoria's Secret. Once the long weekend was over, I went to my home, Bob went to his. No strings, no issues. Just a fun weekend!

My next Sugar Daddy I never met in person. He only asked for pictures of my breasts and feet and another $300 gift card rolled in.

Travel Agent was still in the picture as we were still working together. Him at his agency and me for the cruise line. When I wanted to change jobs, he let me put his company on my resume as if I had worked there. He vouched for me and gave me a stellar review for my next position.

Let me say, here and now, I do not regret any of this. When I went looking for a sugar daddy, I went specifically to be taken care of, mentored, and loved. When I figured out that I was the true one in power, I used that power to my advantage.

It made sense to me gradually. I do not regret anything. Everything was a lesson in the power of my mouth, vagina, and hands for massage, and clearly, my listening skills are what seem to turn these men on. I was the one in power. I no longer needed that father figure. I had learned to take care of myself.

I started to write erotic stories for my guy friends. Of course, I never wanted a critique back. These were just for fun and kept my body to myself, They could have my imagination but my vagina was mine to give out as I pleased, not as they required. If someone asked for it, often at this point, the answer was no.

I did learn that sex was not always on the table and I liked that. I gave massages, I shaved men, more massages and if anything I just listened to them. So many times men just wanted to talk, they wanted to be heard by a woman. I was more than happy to lend them an ear. And, receive that gift card.

I sent videos of myself masturbating, and pictures of my body parts, and wrote more stories. My heart was never engaged. My body and mind might have been but in doing all of this, I was in control. I was in charge of my body and of taking care of myself in a way no other man could at that time.

One guy needed help writing an email to am ex. Nothing difficult. No skin-to-skin contact. I helped, and I got the gift card.

I always liked giving massages. It made me feel like I had power over the men. Yes, sometimes they were massages so some type of sex was involved. Not all the time, but being in control was what I needed at that time. Once I had miscalculated a non-attraction with one man and he insisted on using lavender oil. To this day, that scent makes me ill. It was not worth the gift card on that one. I also made the mistake of having him over to my mom's house when she was not there, of course. It all just seemed wrong to me. I lived and learned. I learned what I didn't want and what made me feel uncomfortable. I remember when it was over, I took the sheets off the bed and threw them directly into the garbage. Never saw him again.

One man booked me on a cruise. Okay, he booked me on three cruises, one a year for a while. I had my own cabin so I was safe. We never had sex. He wanted to but I refused. We did lots of other things but he was never in my vagina. I loved making him orgasm, I loved having control of the ship when he didn't need me. I saw shows and enjoyed all the restaurants. He and I would also spend time together, enjoying the ship. I would give him full-body massages then send him back to his cabin. Three trips, no intgercourse. He paid for everything.

Another man would want me to just jack him off. I loved that control over him. I controlled his orgasm. It gave me such power.

Looking back, yes I know any one of them could have flown me wherever, taken me wherever and just murdered me. This is what I call a charmed life. I came out unscathed and flush with money, gifts, and an amazing life experience.

I do still talk to Travel Agent. Talk only. We've remained friends all these years.

With all this sex in my life, I still thought about becoming an adult performer. I even talked with my mother about it and she said flat out 'no'. What else would she say? Also during all this, I still had major anger toward my non-existent father. I always wondered if putting myself in harm's way was my way to catch his attention. Being with all these men, on my terms or not, was in a way thumbing my nose at my father and his love of the industry. Here I was doing almost the same thing but not on camera. It would have been such an easy move. I looked good, I felt good, I was in control of my life. Or, thought I was.

of course, I wanted a father. Wanted. I wanted someone who was going to pick me up on the weekends and attention to me and, you know, make me breakfast in the morning and talk to me about boy-friends, and work. Talk to me about anything. Just talk to me! And, you know, the fact that he didn't want a title. So, I got that attention from a website with men willing to give me exactly what I wanted.

Yet, for some random reason, my father was being interviewed with Ron Jeremy regarding the condom bill.

"You want to come to this?" My father called and asked me. I heard myself saying yes. After all I had done to distance myself from the man when my father snapped his fingers, I came running.

The meeting was at a major adult company. The waiting room was draped in white curtains and the white furniture gleamed as we waited. Then we were led through glass doors, down a thick blue carpeted hallway to the conference room. More blue and white and silver and awards lined the back wall. In the middle of the large table was water and fresh fruit. Everything was very proper.

I sat in this white conference room and listened to my father talk about condoms in the industry. His babble was somehow mesmerizing yet as he kept going, I found all I wanted was to get out of there. My chair kept inching towards the door. I still have no idea why I was even asked to be there, I suppose I lent some sort of legitimacy to the whole proceeding. I knew at that moment, I would never ever become a performer.

I remember Ron being sweet and trying to make things work for my father and I.

"He is your dad. You should try to reconnect." Ron said softly before the meeting started. I looked at him like he had three heads.

After the meeting, radio silence from Dad resumed.

It was at that moment I also realized, I no longer had daddy issues. I simply let them drop from my hand like letting go of a doorknob to a room you never need to go into. Ever. Again.

8. How I Met a Movie Director

The first I heard about a feature film about my father, I didn't buy it. Bill wasn't famous outside of the adult world or anything so why was his name even out there in the mainstream? A little internet digging and I found out something very weird.

Seems Quentin Tarantino, at the tender age of 16, worked as an usher at a Pussycat Theater. He had dropped out of school in the 9th grade and had to find a job. After a few odd things here and there, he was tall enough and looked old enough to fake his age and get the job at the theater. He watched the films and studied them like any aspiring film student when given access to free materials. Porn or not, Quentin studied. My father took Quentin out for lunch and chatted away about movies with him for two hours. Bill saw Quentin as a lost soul who needed guidance so naturally, Bill stepped in to provide wisdom. Years later when Bill trashed virtually every single movie Quentin ever made (Bill had no recollection of their past interaction) Quentin said he "wouldn't have had it any other way".

It was April of 2023. I was taking several deep breaths having watched my aunt pass away from heart issues in October of 2022. Then dealing with selling her condo in Glendale. My 9-year-old daughter was giving me a run for my money. I knew that eventually, she would need to be put on medication for ADHD. I had been out of work for over a year and had been applying everywhere I could. I had made friends with a lady named Lily who was a friend of Bill's. I got an email from Lily on April 17, 2023, it was titled <u>Tarantino Hints That 'The Movie Critic' is Based on William Margold and "Won't Be A Revenge Story"</u>. I laughed out loud so hard reading this article I hurt myself.

My first reaction was shock. My brain kind of skipped and I thought 'What the hell?'. How does Tarantino even know about Bill?

Of course, he doesn't know about Bill or even who he is or was. This is ridiculous. I got on Reddit and there it was all these people discussing my dad and this other writer like they were famous again. There were multiple threads about the movie and speculation about the subject matter. Were these men even real? Oh yes, they were. Or had been.

I laughed and called my sister.

"You remember Jonny?" She asked.

"Yes, I do," I said. He was a nice guy, maybe a little strange who hung out at my mom's house sometimes. Johnny had a drinking problem and Bill, of course, had to save him. They met in 1962 at Santa Monica City College. Johnny needed saving so Bill brought him on to be a writer at the Hollywood Press. Enter QT. He discovered these two writers that wrote for a trashy porn paper that had mainstream movie reviews which he read when he was younger.

In the middle of my brain meltdown, Lily managed to contact one of Tarantino's agents.

Tarantino's book *Cinema Speculation* invokes Bill's name in it twice. He quoted my father on a made-up word 'revenge-a-matic'. It is supposed to describe a revenge movie but with all the usual and expected things. Like a plot machine that churns out what the audience wants from that kind of movie without many surprises.

Eventually, I get connected with Mike Simpson, Tarantino's agent. As an agent, he gives me the usual spiel. *'If he's interested, he'll get ahold of you.'* With that, I gave him my email and he sent my request to Tarantino. I am Bill's daughter after all. If you are doing a movie about my father, I think I'd like to know something about it.

Time passes and I almost forgot about even talking to Mike when I get a response in my email box. From Quentin Tarantino.

THE Quentin Tarantino. I'm like, no, no, no, no, no. Fantastic. He said he had no idea Bill even had children and he would live to chat on the phone. One issue, he was in Isreal at the time. I'm trying to do all these time zone calculations so we can set up the right time, a few emails fly back and forth. I try to live as normal a life as possible and I think *I am setting up a time to talk to Quentin Tarantino. Sure. This is my life now.*

When my phone finally does go off, I don't answer right away. Why? I was getting my teeth cleaned. I'm trying to just be as normal as possible and I'm in the hygienist chair with instruments being poked into my mouth but Tarantino is calling.

Between plaque scraping and whitening, I answer the call.

"Hey, I am actually getting my teeth cleaned right now," I say. The hygienist waits patiently for me to hang up.

"Cool, cool. Email me when you can so we can try again to talk." QT says and hangs up.

I put the phone down and looked at the girl in the flowered scrubs.

"Sorry, had to take that. Quentin Tarantino. We've been trying to chat for a while." I say casually and put the phone back in my purse. Her eyes were as wide as saucers.

"Lady, you could have gotten out of the chair." She says, not joking. I shake my head no and laugh a little.

"No, my teeth mean way more. I spent way too much money on them." I explain and lay back down for her to finish the work.

At this point, I'm back on Reddit looking up all I could on this movie the man is planning about my father.

Tarantino had been talking about this other writer. Who is this other writer? The internet seems to think it was a fake name my father used when he wrote movie reviews. Others speculate it was some bisexual porn guy who never really came out and gave bad reviews to all porn films. I knew these theories were wrong.

Tarantino explained later that he and a guy with a van would drive around to all the newspaper kiosks in Los Angeles. They would pick up the old porn magazines and restock with the new. Tarantino was introduced to the Hollywood Press.

Since this is all speculation, I want to make sure the man is writing about the right guy. I send him two pictures. One of this other writer and one of my father. He says yes, the other writer is the main character. Still was bizarre to me that my father's name was even near this whole project. Tarantino says again, that making this movie is just speculation.

The Writer's Strike hits that summer and the process comes to a grinding halt. We are still emailing back and forth to try and find a time and place to meet up. Before I knew it, October of 2023 came, and yet another email popped into my Gmail. By this time my friends are telling me to stop talking to him.

Then boom, he's doing the movie, it's no longer speculation. He has the funding and green light from the studio.

Finally, June of this year,(2024) he says *let's meetup*

We agreed to meet at the Pantry in downtown LA which was Bill's favorite place. The Pantry brings back so many childhood memories for me because of their T-bone steaks, coleslaw, pasta, butter, and bread rolls. The older gentlemen dressed properly as waiters with starched white shirts and black bow ties give it an air of a time long gone by. In front of the cage where you pay, cash only, the floor tile is worn through and you see the floorboards. You can still buy gum and grab a toothpick as you get your change.

The plates are those thick diner plates piled with mountains of food. When you eat at the Pantry, you need to arrive hungry. It opened in 1924 and runs 24 hours a day. Since the pandemic, it's augmented its hours but plans on being 24/7 again soon.

Often there is a line outside to wait to get a table. There are no reservations and everything is first come first served. As I waited in line, two gentlemen behind me offered to buy me lunch if my friend didn't show up. They warned me that their conversation might be shocking.

"My father was a porn star and my mother was a social worker. I'm good with any conversation." I smiled. "Nothing could shock me."

Then I spotted QT across the street and he waved. Once the light turned, he crossed and joined me in the waiting line. When he was recognized, he shook hands and accepted the 'love your work' praise politely.

We are eventually led to our table. Steak and eggs for him scrambled eggs and toast for me. The two polite gentlemen are seated behind us. They are slightly shocked that my lunch companion is Quentin Tarantino.

"So how has this changed you or has it with your friends?" QT asks. Meaning how did I handle the fact that my father was a porn star.

One, I'm amazed QT is out with me in public. Two, I'm amazed that he's just spewing stuff, you know, about his movie. Three; people come up, they interrupt, no pictures, but they're like, Hey, can we shake your hand? No problem. We love your movies. Thank you. Again, graceful and with no ego. He is glad to meet people who like his work.

I'm like, cool, let's keep talking. Great, great, great, great. Yes, I am trying not to freak out in my head with the fact that I am eating dinner rolls with Quentin Tarantino at the Pantry. I got this.

Our waiter delivered the food and stopped to look at my lunch partner.

"You know, you kind of look like Tarantino." He says as if this is news.

"I get that a lot." Tarantino smiles.

"Are you him?" The waiter hasn't moved.

"Yeah, I'm him." He confesses. More autographs and smiles and 'love your work' conversation.

Once we parted ways, we shook hands and I watched him go back to his car. Last I heard the movie was being scrapped.

I hope it wasn't something I said.

I will probably never hear from him again.

9. All About Bill

"Part of the tragedy of Bill was that he defined himself by what he needed rather than by what he loved."

PATRICK PALMER
Host of Jizz Talking

I wanted to attend my first Adult Video News show in Las Vegas. Bill says: *'Don't buy the VIP shit, that's just a waste of money. It's a waste of money. It's a money grab for those people, blah, blah, blah'.* But as a first-timer, it's what I do. I bought it anyway.

Bill said *'Take my number down and feel free to call me anytime'.* I am not big on bugging people. Then Bill says *'Let's move onto a different topic. Your email address says something about the Yankees. That must mean you're a Yankee fan'.*

I say of course I am. He asks who is my favorite Yankee. I say Sparky Lyle, a relief pitcher in the 70's. We talked a little bit about Sparky. I ask who's his favorite Yankee? Bill assures me that I have never heard of him. He's an old-time relief pitcher with Coke bottle bottom glasses.

His name is Ryne Duren. I tell Bill I actually met Ryne twice. He passed away a couple of years ago, he was a recovering alcoholic. However, I did get Ryne's autograph.

Bill said; *'Kid, we're going to be good friends'.*

When I did meet him in Las Vegas at his booth at the AVN Show, I also gave him an autographed picture of Don Larsen. It was from a game that got him hooked on the Yankees as a kid. Bill loved that and started crying. Then I understood how tender-hearted Bill was.

DAN MILLER
Editor-in-Chief at AVN Media Network

I was brand new to the adult industry and very hungry to immerse myself in the community. The first industry event that I went to was a Saturday morning. I had been talking to Bill about PAW. They were having a softball game in Long Beach. It was quite a drive on a Saturday morning. I wrote a story about the game to preview it to say it was happening. That's how I knew about it. Bill invited me to come out and check it out. It was the first event I ever attended in adult as a representative of AVN.

I just remember there was nobody there except for the people that were playing, the adult industry personalities. Nobody was sitting in the stands or watching the game.

I get there and sure as anything, Bill is in the announcer's booth by himself like he's announcing the game. I end up sitting next to Bill in the announcer's booth for the whole game and that's where I sort of, you know, got some of the background about what was happening.

Afterward, I went down to the field where I did some interviews and this was barely six weeks into my career in adult. Bill was just having a blast that day. I remember he was the life of the party, so to speak, in the announcer's booth.

That was one of my early impressions of this industry as a community. Bill welcomed me at that time as a new person in this adult world. He was willing to share his wisdom and introduce me around to other people.

So that's really the strongest memory I have about him.

DOMINIC ACCERA
Photographer and Videographer

I was never, ever a great photographer by any stretch of the imagination in the beginning. I started networking with girls because

I would give them copies of the pictures I took of them. At some point, I met Bill but as a fan. I even got his autograph.

So fast forward to when I started working for this thing called Video Excitement. It was a newspaper. They allowed me to basically be a journalist. But everybody in the business said '*You're that little fanboy, you ain't shit*'.

Bill was the first person to take me seriously. He got me into gigs I don't think I would have gotten into without him. He showed me certain things, how certain things went and how certain things didn't, which at that point I was so green and stupid, you know, I didn't know a lot of things.

I think the first time I actually worked with Bill was at the Santa Monica Pier. The old XRCO show about 1989. Bill made sure I had a place on the red carpet to take pictures.

What I learned about Bill was Bill gave a shit about performers more than anybody. He took a ridiculous amount of shit for that.

JEFFERY DOUGLAS
Free Speech Coalition Board Chair
Attorney - Los Angeles, CA

"Part of the tragedy of Bill was that he defined himself by what he needed rather than by what he loved."

Bill was not a member of the board, but characteristically he was in all board meetings. Nobody invited him to come. As one board member said to me, it's more trouble to kick him out. It is easier to just leave him there.

It was a relationship that the powers that be in the industry had towards Bill was ambivalent. That is they felt there were some good things that he did and he was certainly close to being central to the adult performer community.

There were 400 people that made a full-time living acting in the movies. It was a real community. Bill was really close to Jim South. Jim South was by far the dominant talent. Bill spent an enormous number of hours every week in Jim's office. With that, Bill was regarded as being someone who had insight into the population.

Around 1995, interest was sort of lost for the Free Speech Coalition. There was no interest in the organization. There weren't enough nominations to fill the board. An election was impossible. Instead, the annual meeting in Las Vegas coincided with the AVN show, there was a general meeting for the Free Speech coalition members. Thirty or so people in that audience, in a theater that sat, you know, several hundred. So it's obviously a very small crowd. Bill said this is the slate that I endorse. These are the people who should be on the board. He picks a number of his friends, a couple of whom had little to do with, one of whom basically had nothing to do with the adult industry. But they were people who were his close friends.

Another time, Bill was having a fight with another board member. It was at a board meeting. I was not physically in the room. Lenny Friedlander, who like Bill, could be very alpha male. They literally, when they were disagreeing about something, they talked about pulling their dicks out and measuring them to see which one was bigger. Lenny was the owner of one of the largest distributors in the United States, New Beginnings. He was very successful. Although he and Bill agreed on a bunch of things, Bill felt that his success made him an enemy of the people. He also had a personal vow of poverty and contempt for economic success.

Lenny, who was a close friend of mine, said to Bill that he, Lenny, controlled my vote and that I would do anything that he told me to. From that day forward, Bill decided that I was Judas and he turned his remarkable capacity for hate on me. Because someone else said that they controlled me.

I'm trying to remember what year it was that Bill resigned. But what happened was we finally hired a professional executive director. Up until the first five years or more of the coalition's existence, we had one person on staff. She did the bookkeeping and reminded people to pay. Bill hated her. We decided that we could raise enough money to hire an executive director. It was super positive. Step forward. We hired Kat Sunlove.

She was desperately trying to get the big players to come back into the industry to support the Coalition. Notably Vivid and VCA. Ironically, it was Hustler who told her that they would under no circumstances support the Free Speech Coalition if Bill Margold was on the board. She told Bill this in front of the rest of the board. She said, '*Bill, you are the greatest burden this organization has.*"

He said '*Okay, I'll leave*'. Of those five or six companies that told her that Bill was the reason they weren't going to donate, only two of them did donate anyway. Bill took it as a sort of an assassination. He compared himself to Cesar. When he says he quit the organization in order to save it, there's, you know, there's a perfectly valid interpretation of it.

I saw his extraordinary creativity and his deep and meaningful commitment to the well-being of talent. As far as PAW, he couldn't run an organization to save his life. I mean, he just didn't have the skill set and didn't have to follow through. Certainly couldn't solicit donations because he broadcast his contempt for the people who had the money.

His motivations were entirely sincere.

PAUL FISHBEIN
AVN Founder
Free Speech Coalition Board member
Plausible Films producer/director

I joined the Free Speech Coalition board in 1991. That's when I was on the board with him. He was a pretty active free-speech vocalist.

He ran for the board and won. He felt like he was representing the talent on the board.

I think his intentions were always good, but he was the most competitive guy you can imagine. He would fight with people. With the Free Speech Coalition, everybody's on the same page. Everybody's there for one thing, the preservation of the First Amendment, the preservation of people's right to choose and watch what they want in their own home.

I thought he hated me, but seemed to appreciate the fact that we recognized his girlfriend (Viper) as a talent. I actually called some companies on his behalf to say '*You should hire her. She's really good*'. I think he was appreciative of that. I know there were mixed feelings about him from people.

There were some people that loved him and swore by him. Then there were other people that just just hated him. Yeah, that's pretty much the adult industry when it comes to anybody, you know?

PETER WARREN
Managing Editor at AVN Media Network

The story that sticks out the most in my mind is I remember seeing him at Christian Mann's memorial. He asked me, was I covering this? I said I think somebody else is covering it for us. But he said to me, '*You're the damn porn historian. You have to cover this*'. I was like, am I? All right.

He certainly knew who I was.

When he died, he literally dropped dead in the middle of doing his radio show. It was on the first day of our show in Vegas. Word started filtering around and everybody was whispering to each other. Is it true? We're one day one of our busiest week of the entire year, kind of scrambling and running around, trying to grab people for quotes and put a story together as fast as we could and get it out. Timing, right? Yeah.

He always had good timing.

IAN JANE
Owner of https://rockshockpop.com/

Basically what happened was, Bill signed up for the message board on DVDmaniacs.net and I recognized the name because I was familiar with his work. I was like, I wonder if that's the same Bill Margold. So, I asked him are you THE Bill Margold? He wrote back and said, Yep, I am. I asked if I could email him some questions and do an interview for the site. I'd send over a Word Doc, he could fill it out and send it back.

He said, 'Hey, if it's okay with you, what I would like to do is record it like on VHS and just I'll send you the recording and then you can transcribe it." I kind of got the impression he was not super computer-savvy and didn't want to spend a ton of time writing it. So I agreed.

A couple of weeks later I got a message from him saying, Hey, what's from your address, I'll send you the tape. A few days after that tape showed up and the first part of the interview started in the middle of the tape.

Basically the first half of the interview was the last half of the recording. So I had the last half of the tape, which was the first half of the interview, and then had to rewind all the way to the beginning to get to the second half of the interview.

It was kind of strange way to do it. He said he had a friend of his helping with the recording. He was surrounded by teddy bears the entire time when he was on camera. Looked a little a little shaky, looking like, you know, he was older at the time. He answered some of the questions very honestly. I transcribed the interview and that was that. It went up on the website. Once DVD Maniacs folded, I moved it over to Rock Shock Pop.

The one thing that stuck out? It was the teddy bears. So I was like, okay, what is this? This guy is a senior citizen at this point sitting on a couch, talking about the good old days of porn, literally surrounded by teddy bears.

I was like, this is kind of weird. He explained what they were for and the PAW organization but it was still weird. It was a very strange visual contradiction, in a way, to what he was talking about. It just seemed to me that like, you know, you always associate teddy bears with innocence and stuff like that, not porn.

Another thing I remember very vividly about the tape is when he was talking about his relationship with Viper. He started crying. He was absolutely tearing up and getting choked up when he was talking about what happened at the end of their relationship and stuff.

He came across as very egotistical, he was clearly, clearly very happy to be sitting down and talking about himself for 2 hours. But at the same time, there did seem to be an obvious layer of sensitivity to him. He didn't hide the fact that the ego was there. Again, you know, he was more than happy to talk about his career. But underneath all that, you know, I kind of got a sense of sadness, especially when he was talking about Viper and the whole teddy bear thing, and him trying to better the adult industry.

David W. Wahl, Ph.D., ABS
Asst. Professor of Sociology & Criminology
Institutional Review Board, Chair
McMurry University

I said I knew him in the last year of his life.

We had gotten to know each other very well. We're both kind of major film buffs. The first time we met, he was grilling me on movies and he couldn't trip me up. He was always trying to trip me up on movie trivia. It's not possible. Then we started arguing, no matter what movie, no matter what I said about the movie, good or bad, he immediately took the opposite position. It was obvious that he was automatically taking the contrary position.

We were going to have a movie review podcast together and we're going to probably start that, you know, within the next couple of months. At the time I was living in Minnesota. He was living in California, but I mean, you can do that for a podcast. Then, of course, he passed away.

He loved it when people hated him. He relished in it. I was working on a documentary and I asked Bill if he could throw in his $0.02 and he said, sure. I said I need about 20 minutes of your time. That's all I need. He said, '*Let's just do it in my apartment*'. I brought a film crew up to his apartment, got everything set up, and started rolling.

Three hours later, looking back, it was almost like he knew he didn't have much time left and he wanted to get everything out because it was a complete history lesson on the life of Bill Margold. He went into things that he hadn't talked about before.

That was the first time I heard about his kids at all. I heard the interview with him before where he was asked if would he allow his kids to go into porn. He said, yes, of course he would. By the way, I can't remember if at the time I thought that that was hypothetical, if he had kids, or because he didn't talk directly about them.

This was the first time he talked directly about them. But really, the only one he talked about was Juliette. He said some very nice things about Juliette which I imparted to her afterward.

He only specified her. That's the first time I heard about Juliette. I didn't know she existed. She was the one who got the Goldie Bear moniker.

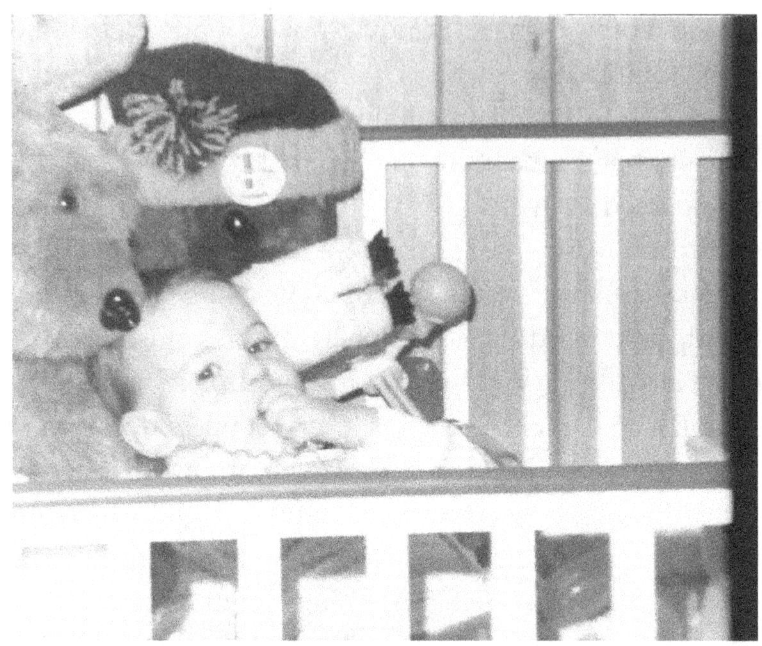

Me in my crib

Mom
OVER THE YEARS

11. Life Without Father

I don't filter my daughter. I've told her what her what her grandfather did for a living. Bill did want to meet her but I was paralyzed at the thought. Nothing bad ever happened to me but some sort of fierce protective gene took over and I never wanted my daughter to meet him.

I have always been upfront with my daughter. I am raising her the way my mother did, with honesty. My daughter is very understanding. We have frank talks about periods and sex, we do not have a filtered household.

Yet, with that, when I knew she was looking up penis pictures on the internet, I wasn't that thrilled. She asked me numerous times about sex and I have been as open as possible. We have discussed masturbation, we call it self-soothing. I just told her to do it in her room, keep the door closed, and wash your hands afterward.

With that, my father's reach is still a thing. Even though she never met the man and he is not gone, people still judge to this day. For some reason, people still think I was molested or that something bad happened to me sexually as a child. They think I am passing that pain on to my own daughter. Nothing could be farther from the truth.

Still, I have been reported to child services three times. My daughter was never taken away but the allegations were thrown at me and my family.

Why?

Because my father was a porn star.

The first time it happened I was pretty blindsided. It was a fairly typical day, picking up my daughter from school, grocery shopping, and planning dinner. While my daughter handled her homework, I got the message. Someone reported me for sexual molestation and neglect. Of course, they did this anonymously. Seems everyone thought I had been molested so naturally my daughter had been. As far as neglect, my daughter wants for nothing in this world. Warm bed, fully stocked fridge, loving parents. It was an insane threat and handled with one phone call.

I explained that my father had been an adult performer.

"Ohhhh, I see." I heard on the other end of the call and it was over quickly.

I know how to handle the Social Services system. I grew up with my mother's job always in my face so I knew these allegations were baseless. I remember having to call three days in a row until I finally got someone to tell me the truth. There were no allegations. There was nothing to report. My father was a porn star, end of story.

With that report, I knew more were coming. Once you were in the system you stayed there. I knew there would be a follow-up call within six months and sure enough, it came. I was ready for it.

Yes, my daughter is still safe. Yes, she is still fed and going to school. No, no one has molested her. No, my father has not come back from the grave to spread evil porn all over my family. We are just fine. Have a nice day.

I went through supervisor after supervisor only to find out, yet again, no one could find any real allegations. They simply stamped my family with the words 'Porn Star' and that was enough for them. Again, I waited.

With the way I talk to my daughter like an adult, when she goes to school and does the same, I am branded as the bad guy. We don't tip-toe around frank questions. If my daughter has questions about sex, I don't lie to her because society thinks she is too young for things. I am her mother and I make those choices. She asks, I answer to the best of my ability. If I don't know the answer, we research it together. I want her to be able to come to be before she goes to Google.

Now, was I happy to find out she was looking up genitals on the internet? No. She has her own curiosity because she is young and growing. Her mind is simply growing faster than some of her classmates.

No matter if other parents want to believe it or not, their kids are doing the exact same thing. Parents cannot be blind to the fact their kids are looking up things they know their parents would not approve of. Why do you think they do it instead of coming to you? It is a matter of trust. My daughter trusts me and knows she can ask me anything. I will never tell her no. If I feel she is too young to learn something, I will be honest and tell her just that. Then check her browser history where she is going to look it up anyway.

I have always wanted to be a mom. I never knew when exactly it was going to happen but when I came back from all my travels and settled back in the States, I knew I was ready. I never actively looked for a father for my child or the man of my dreams. I went back to work here and simply enjoyed my life, my time with my mother, and happily went through my life.

Then on a cool day in November, I was going for a walk to clear my head. It was truly time for me to sort out my thoughts from my workday. I walked past a house and saw a man on the front porch drinking a beer. Also on that porch was a beautiful Husky.

"Pretty dog. What's his name." I asked with a smile.

"Dude. What's yours?" The man smiled.

One year later, our daughter was born.

I had babysat for so many years and yearned for another person in my life who was truly mine. She came out a little jaundice and breastfeeding was challenging. But I had my mother to help me through. I took 15 months off my career path. While I was pregnant, I was so anxiety-ridden it was a little off the charts. I would go down rabbit holes about stillbirth since my daughter originally tested positive for Down's (which she does not have). When she was born, I didn't feel that immediate bond. I only felt a near-crippling fear and wondered how I was going to raise her!

Again, my mom and husband pulled me off the ledge and we all got through just fine. More than fine. My daughter is smart and beautiful.

The actual first time I had a call from Social Services was when she was 2 ½. She was attending a high-end preschool in West LA and she had gotten a dog bite (not from Dude). It was Memorial Day and naturally, I rushed her to the ER. Poor thing was more scared than hurt, shaking like a leaf and crying. Some meds and a quick once over and she was fine. Tears dried, we were home soon and life went back to normal.

I dropped her off at school the following day and noticed two ladies sitting by the drop-off lane, waiting. Seems they were waiting for me.

"Would you come with us?" One of them asked so sweetly I could have barfed.

Shocked, I followed them to an office inside. Once we were all seated and all the smiles had been given out, I was told why I was there. They wanted to talk to me about possible physical abuse towards my daughter. My first thought was 'Who dared lay a hand on my kid?' then I realized, they were staring at me.

I had to defend myself and realize at that point how vulnerable some of my mom's clients must have felt when she had to visit them. I had to sit there and justify my parenting to these two accusing strangers. it was very traumatic for me. The social worker interviewed both my husband and me and then closed the cases. Little did I know what was to come.

After my mom passed away in March of 2017, I had lost a sense of myself and just sort of wandered through life for a long time. My husband and I thought a change of scenery would be the best thing for the whole family. We started to look for a place in Temecula, approximately 85 miles south of Los Angeles. We looked at over 40 houses until we found our dream house in February of 2020. We closed escrow on March 26. Thirteen days after lockdown.

The neighbors seemed welcoming and the neighborhood was quiet. Briefly, I was happy again.

Then the texts started from a neighbor. It was nasty. When I saw the words 'porn star' I fell into a deep depression and returned to therapy for help. I might have moved from Los Angeles, but my father's legacy had followed. Funny, I don't remember adding that to one of the moving boxes but here it was in my life again.

My daughter attended a private school at the time and I quickly moved her to another one. It didn't take very long to have that knock on the door and other side, two well-meaning social workers. I had been reported again. The reason? You already know it. I still felt gut-punched when I had to explain myself all over again. What triggered it this time? Someone heard me swearing. My daughter was in the area as I was swearing. How dare I.

Oh, we are not done.

As I said, once in the system, forever in the system.

In October 2024, I drove to pick up my daughter from school. She climbs into the back of the car, buckles her seatbelt, and settles in for the drive home.

"Guess what?" She chirped happily.

"What honey?" I ask as I stop for a red light.

"A social worker came to talk to me today." She smiles. I nearly rear-ended the car in front of me.

"Oh?" I say when I finally find my voice.

"Yep. Guess what for?" She is clearly ready to giggle and I hope she is joking.

"No clue. What now?" I start to drive as the light turns green.

"You let me watch RuPaul's Drag Race." She says, covering her mouth to stifle a laugh.

"You're kidding?"

"Nope!"

We laughed all the way home.

A week later, the 'your father was a porn star' visits start up again. This time with a twist! This time they said my husband was a porn star from the 70's. My husband was born in 1982 so unless he is some sort of time traveler, call the Vatican. Clearly we have had a miracle.

12. Making Amends with my Father

I saw the movie Boogie Nights in London. My friends and I went out nearly every night so it was just something else to do. This night, it was my birthday. We went out, got champagne, and had our usual great time. We decided to top the night off with a movie.

When I walked into the theater, I knew barely anything about the movie. We got the usual popcorn and drinks, still riding the buzz from the champagne. We made our way to the plush red velvet seats and settled in. I was munching the popcorn and giggling with my friends when the movie started. The popcorn suddenly stuck in my throat like rocks.

As I watched the picture flickered on the screen, I watched Burt Reynolds in action I had only one thought…

"That's my dad."

Reynolds's character was really empathetic. He helped people who came into the industry, they lived in his home. Just like my father had done countless times. Now, did my father have a nice house with a pool? No. Did he shoot in a nice house with a pool? Yes. It was enough for me to put my father's face and voice on that screen.

He brought people into the industry and kind of exploited them at the same time. Then, the Julianne Moore character loses her kid and the whole social service thing. It boomeranged my right back to listening to Viper on the phone trying to hang on to her own child. I was just looking at Burt Reynolds, like, *how did you know? How did the director know my dad?*

It was one of the rare things, I think, that showed porn people as real people.

When the movie ended, I cried. I cried and I called my therapist. Even though I had moved so far away and was living my life for myself, my father's reach had grabbed me again. All the questions I thought I had resolved came back to choke me. How many times had he chosen porn stars over his daughters? Just when I thought I was fine. A darkened movie theater reopened wounds I swore were healed.

He always saw porn stars as people who needed him. They needed rescuing. He made that clear on multiple occasions. No matter how many times I reached out, I was not worthy of that hand to pull me up, to stop me from drowning. I will never ever know why and I have to live with that for the rest of my life.

It was my father who needed rescuing. He never got it.

It has been eight years since his death. I thought his death would somehow be freeing but clearly I was wrong. The fact that my mother died so close to that time just kept my world tearing at all the edged. It's taken me a long time to stitch things back together and often I run out of thread. I sometimes think he died selfishly close to my mother. Yes, I know how that sounds.

The last time I'd seen Bill in person was at the Golden Goddesses book release party at the Hustler store in Hollywood. I brought my husband to the event to meet my father. To be honest, the whole exchange is an absolute blur. I know it was busy, people chatting and hanging out. Then my father took the podium to talk about the book and welcome everyone to the event.

I held onto my husband's hand as Bill spoke. There he was. The man I had spent my entire life trying not to reach out to. Yet, here I was with my husband looking for approval. I was looking for the man to just see me. Look at me. Acknowledge me.

Bill spoke about the event, his raspy nasal voice demanding attention as he looked out over the crowd. He was the center of attention. He held the spotlight. It was all my father ever wanted. He called the event "a once-in-a-lifetime experience" full of "a whole lot of love for people that we love."